Egged On
and other poems

Linda Ewles

Published by Linda Ewles
November 2024

linda.ewles@headspring.co.uk

Design and layout by Linda Ewles

Back cover author portrait by Christopher Flook

Images by Shutterstock
www.shutterstock.com

Printed by Greyhound
www.greyhoundprint.co.uk

ISBN 978-0-9570857-4-9

For refugees, asylum seekers, people without a home and those who offer them friendship and help

Profits from the sale of this book will be donated to
Bristol Refugee Rights which runs a Welcome Centre for refugees and asylum seekers
www.bristolrefugeerights.org
and
Caring in Bristol which works to prevent homelessness and provide practical help and support for people without a safe, secure home
www.caringinbristol.org.uk.

Acknowledgements

Special thanks to all the generous and friendly people on the Bristol poetry scene who have encouraged me by providing helpful feedback on my poetic efforts and being a responsive audience whenever I've read my poems, especially at Silver Street monthly poetry readings in Bristol.

I'm grateful to you all, but particularly Colin Brown and Deborah Harvey for their Friday poetry group and especially for keeping my poetry-writing going with emails and zooms throughout the Covid pandemic years.

Grateful thanks also to Julie-ann Rowell and the members of RWW for many years of inspiring poetry writing, and to Matthew Barton for tutoring the Wednesday Poets. Finally, thank you to the Arvon Foundation for their wonderful poetry courses; I attended several which inspired some of the poems included in this collection.

My thanks also to Heather Lister who gave helpful comments on a draft version of this collection and to Sally Bramley for her eagle-eyed proofreading.

Many thanks to Chris Flook for the photo portrait on the back cover.

I'm so grateful to Greyhound Printers who more than lived up to their reputation for being friendly and helpful.

Finally, I'm indebted to my husband Jim Pimpernell who, as always, patiently sorted out the tech stuff I couldn't do.

Contents

Just for Fun

Preamble

I found putting this collection together quite a challenge as I'd written dozens of poems since publishing my first collection in 2015. Which to choose?

I made a long list of those I thought were the best, or simply my favourites. Some had rhyme, rhythm and form such as a sonnet, others were free verse. Some were humorous, some serious. I dithered for weeks over which ones to include.

Then there was the question of how to turn a mixed jumble of poems into a cohesive sequence. I divided them into categories. I'd written a lot about getting older, so those poems went into the *Poet's Progress* section. Others poked fun about coping with life today as an older person, so these became the *Modern Life* section. Some were simply written for a laugh, so they went into the *Just for Fun* section.

I wanted to include some serious poems, but they jarred with the humour in others, so I grouped them together as the *Seriously...* section.

That left just two: one about me, and one about my approach to writing poetry. I've put them here, in this *Preamble*.

I hope these poems resonate with readers. My aim was to produce a collection which is amusing or thought-provoking, or maybe both. Happy reading.

Amalgamated Me

People say just be yourself
but which self shall I be?
The wife, the sister, neighbour, friend,
the writer, gardener, traveller,
the sailor, teacher, diarist,
the Buddhist, Quaker, atheist,
cat-lover, cleaner, cook.

There are myselves at different times:
the traveller to risky places
I can't believe I ever went to,
the single-handed dinghy sailor
I can't believe I ever was,
the dark-haired quite-good-looker
of my younger days,
now wrinkled white-haired oldie
with fewer teeth and creaky knees.

I am a set of paradoxes:
the life-and-soul, the loner,
the cheerful and Les Mis,
enthusiastic, apathetic,
energetic, couch potato,
adventurous and stay-at-home.

I am collected stories
while still a work-in-progress.
My life is an anthology
that's cut-and-pasted into me
and so I am the self I am
and ever more shall be
amen.

Metaphysical Angst

I'm quizzical re *Metaphysical*
so consult the lexicographical
who say it's *Deep and Meaningful*
Many-layered, Metaphorical,
Mystical, Invisible
and certainly *Philosophical.*
It's situation critical
For one who favours the non-metaphysical.

It's not my thing, I'm WYSIWYG,
I'm What You See Is What You Get.
I like to tell it, show it, know it,
I'm no work-it-out-yourself type poet,
no deciphering, no divining,
no decoding or analysing.
I write of the quotidian
not pious Augustinian,
not issues theoretical,
not abstract, intellectual,
but concrete, understandable.

When I read poems Metaphysic
I sometimes think – oh sacrilegious cynic –
it's like the Emperor's New Clothes,
we're being led by poetic nose
(like Modern Art a child could draw
that really isn't clever at all).
Or is it that I'm ignorant,
poetically illiterate?
Or a dimwit philistine?
Is that why I cannot find
lucid meaning, rhythm or rhyme?

So thinking metaphysical
has put me in a tizzycal.
I need to give my brain a rest
from angsty existential quest,
to smile like Buddha and accept
the here-and-now and everyday,
and write of rain and Friday's pay.
I'll muse without much philosophic clue
but nonetheless I think it's true
the answer's (probably) forty-two.

Poet's Progress

Egged On

It's odd

to think I was once an

egg inside my mother, a pin-head egg,

then a double-yolker-always-doubling egg.

Sometimes I've been a beaten egg or a puffed

meringue from white of egg or a bad egg, good egg,

curate's egg or a free range not-quite-organic egg or a

sunny-side-up or an over-easy egg. Sometimes I'll go to

work on an egg, a scrambled, poached or sizzle-fried

egg. Sometimes I'm a coddled egg or a hard-boiled

Raymond Chandler egg, a speckled egg, a posh

quail's egg or I'm duck-egg-blue with

eggshell finish.

Hairstory

I was born with a shock of dark hair
so they said that I looked like a kitten
not bald as a coot
but coochy-coo cute
with my tufty lock tied with pink ribbon.

When at school what I wanted was plaits
and long hair all shiny and straight.
But Mum said *Little girls*
look best with nice curls
so I suffered home perm's corkscrew fate.

In my teens I had acne and dandruff,
greasy mane only washed once a week.
But perm wars were over
I'd hair to my shoulder
but on school days pinned up in a pleat.

In my heyday I spent loads of cash
on lacquer, hair grips and shampoos.
I wore rollers in bed
to create on my head
sixties backcomb and beehive hairdos.

The day that I found some grey hairs
I plastered on henna in spades.
To match my skin wrinkles
I gave my hair crinkles
which flatter the face of the aged.

When grey hairs outnumbered the brown
I let nature take its own course.
The new grey grew bent
with curly intent
wondrous waves with no crimping or force.

Now my mop has turned brilliant white
cut by Vince each six weeks with much flair.
I'm no longer brunette
I'm the silver top set –
and at long last I'm pleased with my hair.

New Homes

My first were bedsits
with dingy hallways, shared bathrooms,
shelves made from orange crates,
a rug from an old fur coat,
posters stuck up with Blu Tack.

Then shared flats,
squabbles in the kitchen,
Who left the dirty dishes?
Loud parties and cheap wine,
orgasms heard through thin walls.

Years later, home ownership,
worries about boilers, the mortgage.
A Victorian terrace
with a cat, matching saucepans,
giant sunflowers grown from seed.

Next a part-converted barn,
roof repairs and field mice in the garden.
A walk across fields to the village pub
with my new husband who cut the grass.
A traffic-jam commute to work.

Towards retirement
a modern town house,
local artists' paintings on the walls.
City centre, ideal for restaurants,
concerts, the doctor's.

Now an apartment for *later living*,
no stairs, downsized, decluttered.
No upkeep anxieties,
a red cord in the bathroom
for emergencies.

Finally, no roof or walls,
just earth and sky.

Houseproud

"There is no need to do any housework at all. After the first four years the dirt doesn't get any worse." — Quentin Crisp

Ahead of her visits I used to vacuum,
polish, plump the cushions
then wait for her eyes to sweep around
before she'd say *It all looks very nice*.

Now I trace my finger in the dust
on the piano lid
and hear her sniff of disapproval
as I think of Quentin Crisp.

I ignore the peas under the sink
but see her on her knees
every week after Sunday roast
scrubbing the kitchen lino.

As I stuff pillows into
crumpled Easy-care cases
I catch the hiss of her iron,
the whiff of fresh laundry.

So I can't help
dusting the piano
when finger marks glare,
mopping the kitchen floor
when the muck is too much,
but I'll never iron sheets
or tea towels
or socks
or knickers
like she did.

Ode to Pills

Their names evoke exotic places:
Solpadeine sunny Spanish beaches
Sennosides boasts mountain passes
Cetirizine's viewed through opera glasses
Atorvastatin has onion domes
Piriton is ballet's home.

Capsules, caplets, tablets, drops
Suppositories for after ops
Sugar-free pastilles for the throat
Vapour rub smelling of creosote
Detox meds for whisky sins
Cream for pimples on acne'd skin.

Tick them all off on your chart:
Ones to pacify your heart
Vitamins to make you perky
Drugs to ease you through cold turkey
Treat your high cholesterol
Or blockage scatological.

Take with water, take with food
Swallow whole and do not chew.
But there are no magic wands
To right your body's many wrongs.
For every ill there is a pill
But many pills bring on an ill –

Cause diarrhoea and constipation
Fuzzy brain and agitation
Opioids lead you to addiction
Even early valediction.
So take with caution, read the notes
And keep on eating porridge oats.

Cauldron Bubble

O spell dispel demonic lumps
that swell beneath my skin.
Make cysts desist, shrink, shrivel,
die, deflate, expel
the foreign fluid trapped inside
those alien cells.

Turn vengeance on
reviled verruca
barnacled to my big toe.
Wizen that wart to certain death
with curse more lethal than
whole tubes full of Bazuka.

May cataracts clear overnight
all cloudy vision vanish.
May 20 / 20 be restored
with eyesight bright again,
so I can read small print once more
my spectacles not needed.

Make joints not creak
nor muscles moan
nor stomach swell
nor bosom droop
nor belly bulge
and waistbands never strain.

Annihilate all ugly signs
of crept decrepitude:
spiders' webs of broken veins,
brown liver spots, grey sag bags
under bloodshot eyes.
Spell doom to all my body's blights!

Conundrum Age

I want to dance the night away
>but also be in bed by ten
I want to rave at Glastonbury
>but never need the loo

I want to wear red Jimmy Choos
>if comfy as my slippers
I want to paraglide and fly
>with feet kept on the ground

I want to helm an ocean yacht
>while basking in a deckchair
I want to see exotic temples
>if Scotty beams me over there

I want to live the life of youth
>I want to stay home safe and snug
I am too old to feel this young
>I am too young to feel this old

Travel Guide to the Afterlife

When you shuffle off your mortal coil
and your sat nav is no use at all
you might consider a route up high
towards celestial blue sky.
But if allergic to fine feathers
you may have trouble in the heavens
where angels moult their wings and sneeze
and chubby cherubs tend to wheeze.

In wintertime at the Pearly Gates
beware of queues where St Peter waits
with brand new halos at the ready
and zimmer frames for the unsteady.
An option for a warmer time
is going south to a hotter clime
but watch for devils cooking roast
and wielding forks to make you toast.

You could pick purgatory of course –
head there if you're the popish sort.
Confess your sins to cleanse your soul,
put money in the begging bowl
so you're not kept too long on hold
while Mozart plays (or so I'm told)
as you await your purification
before your final destination.

Here's what I recommend to friends:
forget about heaven and hellish ends
(designed as opium for the people
thus preventing unpleasant upheaval).
Instead, maybe reincarnation
is more your personal inclination,

reborn into a new condition
(let's hope not as a politician).

But best, I think, is to choose oblivion
in the nothingness meridian,
returning to the absent form
you had before you were even born.
Leave loving footprints and a jolly wake
with whisky, sandwiches and cake
then float away to non-exist
in the vanished bliss of the atheist.

Modern Life

Shakespeare's Smartphone

How I do hate thy phone that bleeps at thee –

thus plaguing honeyed talk at supper time.

I want thy full attention beamed on me –

to read thy emails is a wicked crime.

Yet worse is taking photos of thy food,

or texting what thou seest on thy plate.

That is the very height of manners rude –

it verily doth make me most irate.

But oh! what joy thy Tweets when I'm not near!

To see on Facebook how thy fame hath spread!

To send thee selfies that thou holdest dear!

To speak with thee when thou hast left my bed!

'Tis love and hate close coiled around thy phone,

like thou and I entwined with playful groan.

I-jack

A *mouse* was once a squeaky pest, a *reboot* meant new shoes
Texts were in your schoolbooks and *sleep mode* was a snooze
Mobiles twirled on playroom ceilings, phones stood in red boxes
The *apple store* was where you kept the Bramleys and the Coxes.

Chips were what you had with fish; 'twas fruit, not paper, jammed
Pork luncheon meat for sandwiches was what you knew as *Spam*
A *wireless* was the radio and *Amazon* a river
And *blue tooth* meant that something must have gone wrong with
        your liver.

A *mail chimp* was an alpha ape, a *tablet* was a pill
Clouds were just for storing rain and *tweets* a songbird's trill
A *server* was a waiter and your *mac* kept out the rain
Memory wasn't in a stick but coiled within your brain.

Spreadsheets hung on washing lines, a *cursor* was a witch
A *hardware store* was where you went to buy a new light switch
A *webmaster* was cobweb king at old Miss Havisham's
And *chrome* was what you polished on your Harley-Davidsons.

Language is a living thing, evolving, and that's fine
But messing with the 'I' that's me, at that I draw the line
You see, I'm locked inside an iPad, no way can I get out
My pod is cast, my bytes bite back, I'll crash without a doubt.

I'm pixilated, google-dongled, dropboxed-out, max-apped
It's hell to find that me myself, my soul, my 'I' is trapped
I need my personal pronoun back, I want the 'I' that's me
I've been hijacked by an iPad and I'm fighting to be free.

Bon Mots

My problems are but challenges,
my answers are solutions.
I do not drink a cuppa
but sip on an infusion.
I order latte, cappuccino,
double shot americano
espresso or macchiato
(Never coffee, heavens, no!)

My dwelling is a luxury home
which I aspired to co-own
because it was affordable,
bijou and adorable.
(Cheap and small? No, not at all!)

The décor is in shabby chic,
furnishings bricolage, antique.
Like my attire, the style is vintage,
pre-loved, fitting for my image.
My favourite footwear's pre-owned too,
created by one Jimmy Choo.
(Not second-hand, the word is banned!)

Bon mots pour moi, n'est-ce pas?
Et toi?

Mail Order

I watch the tiny van on screen
creep jerkily towards my house
six stops to go until it's here.
It brings me gifts for which I've paid
with money zapped across the air.

Some things are not as I had thought:
the veg rack with three tiers not two,
the dress that's skimpy, tight and short,
the cork mats not quite thick enough,
the jumper itchy round my neck.

But still there's that faint Christmas feel
of telling Santa what I'd like,
of expectation building up,
of scissors cutting parcel tape,
of hoping this time it's just right.

Potato Waffles

I've never eaten one
but they're probably nice,
crunchy, salty, moreishly tasty.

At the factory
the presenter's eyes bulge
with pseudo excitement
as gargantuan containers
spew out tonnes of spuds.

We see them steamed, mashed,
dehydrated, rehydrated,
churned, flavoured, moulded, coated,
fried, cooled, frozen, palleted,
hauled, stored, shelved, sold.

A marvel of precision engineering,
gastronomic research, complex logistics,
creative enticement to consume.

All that effort
all that energy
all that skill
all that drive
to turn a potato
into a waffle.

People, planet, potatoes
in a cycle of destruction.
I shout at the screen
JUST EAT A POTATO!

Phone Fumes

If you were sorry –
you wouldn't subject me
to twenty minutes
of crap muzak
punctuated
by your lies.

If you cared –
a real live person
would answer
when I scream
Is anybody there?

If I mattered –
your press-button options
would actually include
my reason
for calling.

You say it cuts costs.
I say it costs you
in pounds of ill-will.
And I pay
in shedloads of stress
and cake-loads of calories
every time I hear
We're sorry to keep you waiting.
Your call is important to us.

Purple Pencil

My current one is purple
but they come in many colours,
sold in Smith's in packs of ten
with handy little rubbers on the end.
They're called non-stop because
you turn the end to get more lead.

But it's a lie that they're non-stop.
The lead runs out, they're thrown away.
Made of plastic – that's the problem,
destination landfill mountains,
or floating islands of detritus
eaten by seabirds, fish and turtles.

I've thought of eco-friendly options:
vintage wooden holders topped
with metal nibs to dip in inkwells,
quill pens made for Stratford tourists,
biodegradable plain HBs
you twist to points in sharpeners.

None compares to my plastic pencil.
It fits my fingers, forms my letters,
lets my writing glide across the page,
compiles 'to do' and shopping lists,
makes handy notes on yellow Post-its,
completes the morning crossword.

I eat less flown-in food, no meat,
travel by foot and electric car,
go shopping with my bags-for-life,
don't wrap with clingfilm anymore.
But I write this in smothered guilt,
with my plastic purple pencil.

The Dandelion's Lament

Why aren't I wanted on green lawns?
I'm puzzled that I'm so despised.
Why are daisies made so welcome
but my survival's jeopardised?

The children like me and talk of clocks
as they blow my seeds and watch them fly
but parents reach for poison potions
that make me shrivel up and die.

Chefs make soup from stinging nettles,
add sorrel and garlic to their stews
but they don't savour my special flavour:
I'm not in recipes they choose.

I've a dandy mop-head like a Beatle,
I've roots like lions' claws below
but they leave me out of the Meadow Mix
that's all the vogue at the Chelsea show.

Think again, think of the bees,
the wondrous way I spread my seed.
I'm needed in our ecosystem
as a wildflower, not a weed.

Who'll take on the PR challenge?
Raise my status to *fleur du jour*?
Serve me in dishes for Masterchef
and love me in gardens for evermore?

Grit in the oyster

It's cold calls when your dinner's ready
The tabletop that won't stay steady
The bus so late you missed your train
The key that fell right down the drain

It's painted walls spray-canned by vandals
The doors that don't have any handles
The slugs that eat your precious shoots
The socks that ride down in your boots

It's babies crying for no reason
The trip you planned for the rainy season
The neighbour's faulty car alarm
The politicians' lying smarm

The cat that claws you when you stroke
The egg you fried but broke the yolk
The button lost, the zip that's stuck
The *'sorry, mate, you're out of luck'*

It's things that ought to work but don't
It's want that can't and will that won't
It's rough to counterbalance smooth
It's all those little things that ooze

pearl drops of irritation

Seriously…

Refugee Strawberry

On a cold November day
I smile to see
a strawberry on the pavement.

A fat luscious strawberry,
neat little seeds in its shiny skin,
a frill of green leaves round its stalk.

Perfectly formed, full of promise.

I think of how this sunshine fruit
was picked to travel miles
in punnets, fridges,
ships and lorries,
ripe for eating with cream
to a soundtrack of tennis.

But now it sits alone

on a grey paving stone
to be seized by a gull,
squashed underfoot,
or sluiced down the gutter
by an icy downpour.

Skin Deep

The apples on the fruit stall smile at me
Skins shine with promise of crisp juiciness
But when I get them home I see that some
Are not yet ripe and some are past their peak
And some have broken skin and some are bruised
And one conceals a maggot deep inside.
I use a kitchen knife to peel and slice
Excise those parts I do not want to eat.
I knew a man who ate an apple whole
Not just white flesh but skin and core and pips
And damaged bits so there was nothing left
To be condemned, cut out or shoved aside.
All edible, he said, and smiled as he
Accepted bruises, blemishes, the whole of me.

Night Shift

Bats dart past my window in their dusky search for gnats;

the rattle of the cat flap signals time for evening hunt.

Students close their laptops and stream out for downtown clubs;

burger man fries onions ready for cheap takeaways;

smokers outside Weatherspoons meet up for curry night.

On Park Street nightclub bouncers flex their muscles in black

   shirts

as gangs of Friday night lads on the pull drink lager pints

while wafting heady aftershave and eyeing miniskirts.

On College Green the Council workers put out plastic pissoirs

as homeless men pitch cardboard and damp duvets on the street.

Paramedics brace themselves for lives leached out in gutters;

nurses on night duty head towards the hospital.

As for me, I turn the lights on, draw the curtains snugly tight

and listen to my radio tuned to 'The World Tonight'.

Little Owl

I bought you from a gift shop in Athens –
a little blue owl with wide all-seeing eyes,
symbol of goddess Athena.

In your wisdom, Athena, can you tell me
if gods are human creations conjured
to make sense of sunrise and thunder?
Were you invented
to personify the intangible,
embody lofty aspirations,
be an anchorage,
a means of taming the unruly,
or a path to bliss?

These days I see you swept aside
by tides of human knowledge,
no place for gods
as scientists reveal the secrets
of life in our infinite cosmos.

But I wonder if you truly exist
in a different dimension,
familiar to priests and mystics,
unseen by most of us?

If so, Athena, will you live on
when we no longer inhabit
our overheated Earth?
When all the little owls
have ceased to be?
And will you be weeping
at human folly?

The Jesus Ghost

When I was little
Jesus lived behind sunbeam clouds,
wearing a white nightie
like an angel who didn't need wings.
He sent my aunty a miracle baby
and heard my prayers in Sunday School.
I won a prize
for a plasticine nativity scene.

When I was a teenager,
beset by blackheads and school bullies,
Jesus was my invisible friend.
I talked to him for hours, kneeling
by my bedside, head in hands,
confessing, being forgiven,
being loved and listened to,
safe inside my bible bubble wrap.

In my twenties Jesus left me,
chased away by science
which explained the supernatural.
Real people were my friends,
human counsellors healed.
Notions of sin and salvation
became repugnant, and nobody
rose from the dead on the third day.

But a stubborn religious gene
begat a black hole deep inside.
Nature abhorred this vacuum
so she filled it with wonder
at her creation. I added
ideals of Buddhist lovingkindness,

Quaker ways of peace and truth,
mindful meditation.

I have lived longer
than three score years and ten,
yet even now I often sense
the ghost of Jesus past.
He haunts me still,
in Christmas tingles,
the Hallelujah Chorus
or incredible cathedrals.

But we don't talk anymore.

Imprint

Where will I go when I'm buried or burnt,
my body recycled, my atoms dispersed?

I might become part of a worm or a daisy,
set down in a desert or field of potatoes,
infiltrate the body of somebody else
or be spiralled away to the stars.

I may sink to the floor of the ocean,
to resurface in millions of years
as a fossil trapped tight in a rock
till Earth's time is finally over.

And what of my mind, of my spirit?
That may be recycled too,
to live on in the souls of those people
whose lives I have touched in some way.

I may pass on down for good or for ill
through lives that are yet to be born
like a homeopathic dilution
till the shadowy imprint is lost.

Just for Fun

Let there be fun

Let there be fun
    so the flutter of a tickle
    turns a whinge into a giggle.
    Let children blow soap bubbles
    so rainbows turn the troubles
    of worried sighs to smiles.

Let there be fun
    so corny Christmas cracker jokes
    and paper hats make winter warm.
    Let the Ministry of Silly Walks
    and Gromit's rubber eyebrow-talk
    make farces of pomposity.

Let there be fun
    so leaden hearts float free
    in a flight of bright balloons.
    Let sad steps skip in conga lines,
    dark thoughts dance free like butterflies,
    and black dogs play like Andrex puppies.

Let there be fun
    let's frolic away our dismal days,
    laugh our pessimistic socks off
    so toes are piggy-wiggle free
    and princes won't be frogs again
    and we'll have custard pies for tea.

To Do or Not to Do

My New Year's resolution is
to tackle too much busyness:
I'll not make lists of *Things to Do*.

They merely serve to stress me out
till all the *Things to Do*
are done.

Instead I write a *Don't Do* list of things
that would have been on my *To Do* list
if I'd done one.

But while I write my *Don't Do* list
I worry that the *Don't Do* things
will not be done if I don't do them.

I tell myself that if they stay undone
the world won't stop
and nobody will die.

But still the *Don't Do* things
get tangled tight into a knot inside so bad
it makes me do them.

One by one I tick them off
and feel the knot undo as all
the *Don't Do* things get done.

And all the while I smile because
I kept my resolution:
I did not write a list of *Things to Do*.

Shod

kinky boots, Chelsea boots, plimsolls, clogs
killer heels, Dr Scholl's, hobnails, Crocs
snowshoes, ballet shoes, crampons, pumps

Wellies are necessities
for times when life is shit
when you wallow in manure
tramp ground that's mud-suck heavy
legs bone-weary, soggy socks
all ridden down.

moccasins, sling-backs, Oxfords, sneakers
bootees, Birkenstocks, brothel creepers
slippers, Mary Janes, jellies, Uggs

Sandals are for seasons
when life's a gentle stroll
of sunlight steps on silver sand
pale stripes on sun-bronzed feet
toasted chipolata toes
exposed to barbecues.

army boots, peep toes, flip-flops, mules
lace-ups, espadrilles, Jimmy Choos
deck shoes, court shoes, gym shoes, wedges

Party shoes for shiny nights
chandeliers and celebrations
spiked stilettos on red carpets
platforms swaying, glam sashaying
champagne numbing
your sore toes.

loafers, brogues, Doc Martens, waders
    thigh boots, trainers, winklepickers, flats
        galoshes, gladiators, steel toe caps

    Feet shoed in or booted out
    shod in your extremities
    for all eventualities.

Nonsensicals

What is the sound of one hand clapping –
Is it half a clap or none?
Is it a single hand that smacks
the beat of a semi-heard drum?

What is the smell of a triangle –
is it paper or pencil or chalk?
Or theorems that waft from Pythagoras' brain
or the fumes from isosceles talk?

What is the colour of cheerfulness –
do you see it as strawberry pink?
Or maybe it's sunshiny yellow
you catch now and then through a chink?

What is the taste of your immortal soul
if licked like a child's lollipop?
Is it candyfloss sweet or vinegar sharp,
fiery chilli or fairy dewdrop?

And if you touch air, what is there to feel?
Just a void without sound, smell or taste.
And nothing to see, which is awfully strange
because some things are up there in space:

all the teaspoons, the keys and the socks
that have vanished right into thin air.

How Do I Crave Thee

With apologies to Elizabeth Barrett Browning

How do I crave thee? Let me count the ways.

I crave thee to the depth and breadth and bite

My soul can reach when cake is in my sight

And renders dormant taste buds all ablaze.

I crave thee most when birthday cakes amaze

As serenaded in the candlelight

When scrumptious slices taste of fruit delight

And sweetly iced creations draw my praise.

I crave thee with a passion that I use

In baking Battenburg, banana bread

Eclairs, rum babas laced with tipsy juice.

Dark chocolate brownies, savoured till none left,

Help me to smile through tears; and, if God choose,

I shall eat angel cake beyond my death

God's Biscuits

Sunday school biscuits are jammy dodgers that stick round your
teeth.
Gentle-Jesus-meek-and-mild biscuits are vanilla wafers.
God-of-love biscuits are chocolate cookies, squidgy and moreish.
Vengeful Old Testament ginger nuts need appeasing with a dunk.

The C of E faithful feast on traditional custard creams.
Teetotal Methodists favour Teatime assorted.
Catholics feed on fancy macarons, incense flavoured.
Plymouth Brethren prefer a plain cream cracker.

Quakers consume oatcakes in peace and quiet.
The Salvation Army marches on hard tack.
Evangelicals praise Hobnobs with noisy crunches.
Scientologists revel in nutty biscotti.

Druids share Stonehenge cereal bars.
Pagans relish organic fig rolls.
Jewish matzos are kosher made by Momma.
Buddhists are mindful of Jaffa Cakes, neither cake nor biscuit.

God's immortal invisible divine digestives
dwell in a treasured antique barrel.
Atheistic biscuits are in
an empty tin.

To Send or Not to Send

That is the question as I scan my list.

Whether 'tis nobler in the mind to send

To everyone as usual this time

Including those not seen for donkey's years?

I cross out folk who've left their mortal coil

But what of those who always send to me

Who'll think I've died if I don't send one back?

And others who just sling an email now

Because they need a mortgage for the stamps

And that's the eco-friendly way these days?

O tiresome chore it is to write those cards!

But yet I love to hear the postie call

To feel a glow when I read messages

And think of those who thought of me this year.

Santa's Mints Meet Pies

Mince pies are filled with mincemeat
which isn't mince and isn't meat
and isn't minty like Polo mints
or minty like the Royal Mint.
Mince pies don't mince
but prance and dance like Strictly
quickly down the chimney pots
for Santa Claus who scoffs the lot
but has no claws upon his paws
but does put hoof upon the roof
with his reindeer who don't reign
but are dear to keep and train
and dearly loved but don't like rain
but glow with snow upon their antlers
which don't have ants
but do have sleigh bells
that do not slay
but jingle jangle all the way
helped along by frolicking elves
in Santa's grotto
which isn't grotty
but filled with presents
for the future
up in Lapland
where racing reindeer lap each other
round and round the North Pole
which isn't like a maypole
because it's frozen like in Iceland
which purveys the perfect pies
or so it says in *Which?*
which isn't written by witches
but judged by Bake-Off bakers

who never have soggy bottoms
or shimmy down chimneys
where Rudolph's red nose reigns
and Santa spies those pies